Thank you for a wonderful reunion!
Best regards from
    Inger and Clause

Maja & John
Frild

D0576277

Contents

5

Snow-capped mountains and warm-hearted people. Deep fjords carved into the bedrock. Fertile valleys, enchanting villages and cascading rivers. Glaciers like glistening wisps of cream on unspoilt landscapes. A country of contrasts and drama. The midnight sun, the bustling Oslo streets, the dark season, the coastal steamer, Nidaros Cathedral, idyllic meadows bursting with flowers, and the dangerous polar bears of Svalbard. Warm summer days, stormy seas, 50 degrees below zero, and a nation that has learned to adapt to the forces of nature. This is Norway.

This is Norway

Vestvågøy, Lofoten

HISTORY, CULTURE AND TRADITION

HISTORY

Norway - "the way to the north" - is an appropriate name for the most northerly country in Europe. With its 387,000 km², Norway is Europe's fifth largest country, although its population is only 4.8 million. Norway borders Sweden, Finland and Russia in the east, and the Atlantic Ocean in the west. Archeological discoveries indicate that Norway's first inhabitants settled here at the end of the last Ice Age, about 11,000 years ago. Initially, Norwegians depended on fishing and trapping for their livelihood. Later, they developed ocean-going ships, and became expert seafarers. Military expansion and flourishing cultural development characterized the Viking period (800-1050). King Harald Hårfagre unified Norway as one kingdom just before 900. The Viking kings Olav Tryggvason and St Olav introduced Christianity in about 1000. In the High Middle Ages, the "Norges-veldet" (Norwegian dominion) was a major North European power, and included Iceland, Greenland, the Faroe Islands and parts of Sweden. Norway was united with Denmark from 1380 to 1814, and with Sweden from 1814 until 1905, when it finally regained its independence.

The 5000-year-old rock carvings from Alta are listed as a Unesco World Heritage Site

The statue of St Olav at Stiklestad

The Oseberg ship from ca 850.

The Royal Palace.

THE ROYAL FAMILY

Norway is a constitutional monarchy. The King is the head of state, but has no real political power. Among the people of Norway, however, the royal family has always had a special role as a symbol of the country's independence. Since 1905, the country has had three kings: Haakon VII, Olav V, and the current monarch, Harald V.

Above: The royal family.

Left: The opening of the Storting (parliament).
Below: The Storting.

DEMOCRACY

Today, Norway is a well-developed democracy with comprehensive welfare systems. The country is governed according to parliamentary principles, where the Storting (parliament) has legislative power and the government has executive power.
The Riksforsamling (National Assembly) drew up Norway's constitution at Eidsvoll in 1814.

Roald Amundsen (1872-1928) was an important polar explorer, and led many challenging expeditions. He was the first person to reach the South Pole, where he planted the Norwegian flag on 14 December 1911.

Roald Amundsen

ADVENTURERS WHO OVERCAME BARRIERS

Fridtjof Nansen (1861-1930) was a renowned polar explorer, scientist, politician and humanist. He crossed Greenland on skis in 1888, and from 1893 to 1896 he undertook an epic expedition through the ice of the Arctic Ocean on the polar vessel "Fram". In 1922 Nansen received the Nobel Peace Prize for his humanitarian work.

Fridtjof Nansen

Thor Heyerdahl (1914 - 2002) is the most famous explorer of our time. On his balsa raft, the Kon-Tiki, he allowed the currents to float him from Peru in South America to Polynesia in the Pacific, to prove that the Polynesians could have originated in South America. In the same way, he used the papyrus raft Ra II to prove that people could have crossed the Atlantic in ancient times.

Thor Heyerdahl

WORLD-FAMOUS NORWEGIAN ARTISTS

Three Norwegian writers have received the Nobel Prize in literature: Bjørnstjerne Bjørnson (1832-1910), Knut Hamsun (1859-1952) and Sigrid Undset (1882-1949).

But one of the world's most important dramatists never received this honour. Henrik Ibsen (1828-1906) enriched European theatre with psychological depth and masterly stagecraft. Ibsen's plays are still performed at the world's most famous theatres, and literature researchers regularly publish new books interpreting the dramatist and his plays. "A Doll's House" and "The Wild Duck" are among his finest works. "Peer Gynt" is also well known, especially because of the music that Edvard Grieg composed for this play.

Henrik Ibsen

Edvard Munch (1863-1944) was a pioneer in the art of painting. He wanted to express the innermost feelings of human beings. He painted melancholy and angst, but also the joy of living and love.

Above: "The Girls on the Bridge", oil painting by Edvard Munch.

Edvard Grieg (1843-1907) put Norway on the international music map with his sparkling and vital compositions. A fresh breath of Norwegian nature inspires his work. When you listen to his music, you can visualize the fruit trees blossoming in Hardanger, waterfalls, fjords and mountains. Today Troldhaugen – Edvard Grieg's home, near Bergen – is a popular museum.

Edvard Grieg

NORWEGIAN NATIONAL DRESS

There is growing interest in the traditional, beautiful and colourful Norwegian national dress, or bunad. The costumes are a very popular choice for special occasions such as weddings, baptisms, confirmations, and the National Day. Norway has a wealth of national costumes. Each region has developed its own distinctive design. The bunad is often richly decorated with embroidery and silver jewellery. Traditionally, a man wears a magnificent ornamented knife with his bunad.

Left and above left:
From the Norwegian Folk Museum.

STAVE CHURCHES - A MEDIEVAL HERITAGE IN WOOD

The stave churches are unique and irreplaceable relics of a bygone age. Unesco has designated the stave church of Urnes in Sogn as a World Heritage Site. Historians estimate that Norway once had about a thousand stave churches. Today, only 28 remain. Preserving the stave churches is a high priority for Norwegian conservation authorities. The most famous are the Borgund and Urnes stave churches in Sogn, which both date from about 1150, and Heddal Stave Church in Telemark, dating from about 1250. For the traveller of today, the stave churches are fascinating and exotic vestiges of a remote medieval era.

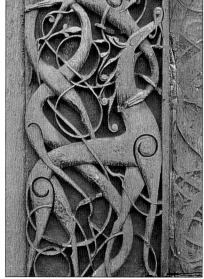

Previous page: Top right: "Hardingfele" (Norwegian fiddle).
Bottom right: Rose-painted chest from Rauland.

Above: Heddal Stave Church.
Right: Detail from Urnes Stave Church.

13

Above: Norwegian salmon - a tempting culinary delicacy.

Left: The fishing grounds outside Lofoten.

Below: Drying fish on racks in Lofoten. Dried Lofoten cod has been exported to many countries in Europe since Viking times.

Above right: Norwegian mountain farm in Sogn.
Below right: Rømmegrøt (sour-cream porridge), fenalår (cured mutton) and flatbrød (thin wafer crispbread).

Below, far right: Tempting Norwegian specialties.

FOOD FROM UNSPOILT NATURE

Norway's coastline extends for more than 21,000 kilometres, and its seas are rich in fish. So fish has always played a central role in Norwegian cuisine.

Unspoilt Norwegian nature and the slow ripening process this far north give unrivalled flavour to fruit, berries and vegetables. The animals that graze on the succulent green grass of the mountains provide meat of outstanding quality.

Take the sea route to Oslo. Enjoy the most beautiful seaward approach that any city could desire. Watch fertile cornfields and smooth, inviting rocks glide past as white sails welcome you to Norway's green capital at the end of the Oslofjord. With its thousand years of history, Oslo offers a glorious intermingling of culture, entertainment and nature.

Experience Norway's national day in Oslo, with the unforgettable procession of children along the street of Karl Johan. Everybody wants to see the Viking Ship Museum, the Vigeland Sculpture Park and the Holmenkollen Ski Jump, but don't forget to enjoy the exhilarating sea breeze and the freshly cooked shrimps at Aker Brygge on the waterfront.

Oslo and the Oslofjord

Oslo, the Opera House

OSLO

Oslo is the capital of Norway as well as its largest city, with a population of about 575,000. The Royal Palace, the Storting (parliament), the government and other central State institutions are all located here. The Vikings founded Oslo in about 1000, and it became the capital of Norway in 1299. Today, Oslo is a modern city with busy shopping districts, a wealth of cultural events and an exiting nightlife. But nature is never far away - forests and sea surround Oslo on all sides.

Below: Aker Brygge and Rådhuset (the City Hall). Above left: Summer mood in Oslo; Studenterlunden Park and Aker Brygge. Above right: Norway's parliament, the Storting. Right: Norway's national day, 17 May — children's procession along the street of Karl Johan.

Karl Johan is Oslo's busy main street, and stretches from the Central Station to the Royal Palace. Between the Storting and Nationaltheatret (the National Theatre), Studenterlunden Park provides a green oasis in the city centre. Overlooking the harbour is Akershus Fortress, Oslo's majestic medieval castle.

Below left: Night in Studenterlunden Park.
Left: Karl Johan Street on a summer evening.
Right: Nationaltheatret (the National Theatre).
Below: Full moon over Akershus Fortress and the full-rigged ship "Christian Radich".

Above: Vigeland Park. Right: Aerial view of a cruise ship in Oslo Harbour, Aker Brygge, Rådhuset (the City Hall). and parts of the city centre.
Below: The Royal Palace and statue of King Charles III John (Karl Johan). Bottom: Oslo Cathedral.

THE OPERA

Like a gleaming white iceberg of marble, Oslo's new landmark rises from the fjord. The new building for the Norwegian Opera and Ballet at Bjørvika is one of the world's most spectacular opera houses, designed by the Norwegian architect firm Snøhetta.

Previous page, top: Tourists on the Opera House roof. Below left: The statue of Kirsten Flagstad. Below centre: Scene from the operetta "Die Fledermaus".

Left: Scene from the ballet "The Nutcracker". Above: The foyer of the Opera House. Below: The Norwegian National Opera and Ballet; evening mood at Bjørvika.

GUSTAV VIGELAND

1869 – 1943

VIGELAND PARK

The Vigeland Park is Norway's top tourist attraction, with more than a million visitors every year. Gustav Vigeland's large sculpture park, unique in the world, portrays the phases of human life from birth to old age. The most famous sculptures are the Monolith, a granite column 17 metres (56 feet) high, and the bronze figure "Sinnataggen" ("Boy in a Tantrum").

Many of Norway's largest and most visited museums are on the peninsula of Bygdøy, west of the centre of Oslo. The most famous are the Viking Ship Museum, the Norwegian Folk Museum, the Kon-Tiki Museum, the Fram Museum and the Norwegian Maritime Museum.

Below: The Kon-Tiki Museum. Left: The Gokstad ship in the Viking Ship Museum. Above: From the Norwegian Folk Museum.

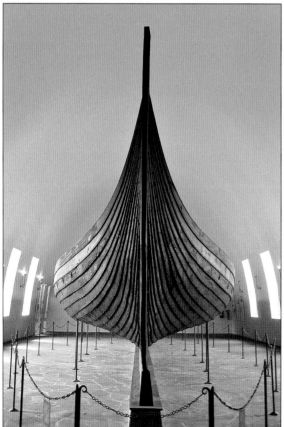

Holmenkollen is Oslo's world-famous ski jump and stadium. The Holmenkollen Ski Festival takes place here every year, featuring skiing events that attract enthusiastic crowds. Since the first Holmenkollen ski jump was completed in 1892, the jump has been changed and extended many times.

Left: Norwegian Folk Museum – Gol Stave Church.
Above and below: The Holmenkollen Ski Jump.

THE OSLOFJORD

The Oslofjord stretches from Oslo to the Færder lighthouse. This is an important transport artery, with many ferries and other ships. The fjord is also a popular recreational area, attracting thousands of pleasure craft in summer. Sailing into the Oslo Fjord, we pass many historical places. To the east is the border town of Halden with the Fredriksten fortress, and Fredrikstad with Gamlebyen, Scandinavia's best-preserved fortress town. To the west is Tønsberg, the oldest city in Norway.

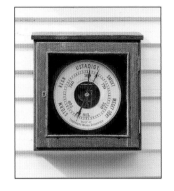

Left: Færder lighthouse.
Below: Tønsberg.

Above: Sailing regatta, Drøbaksundet.
Below: Gamlebyen (the Old Town) in Fredrikstad.

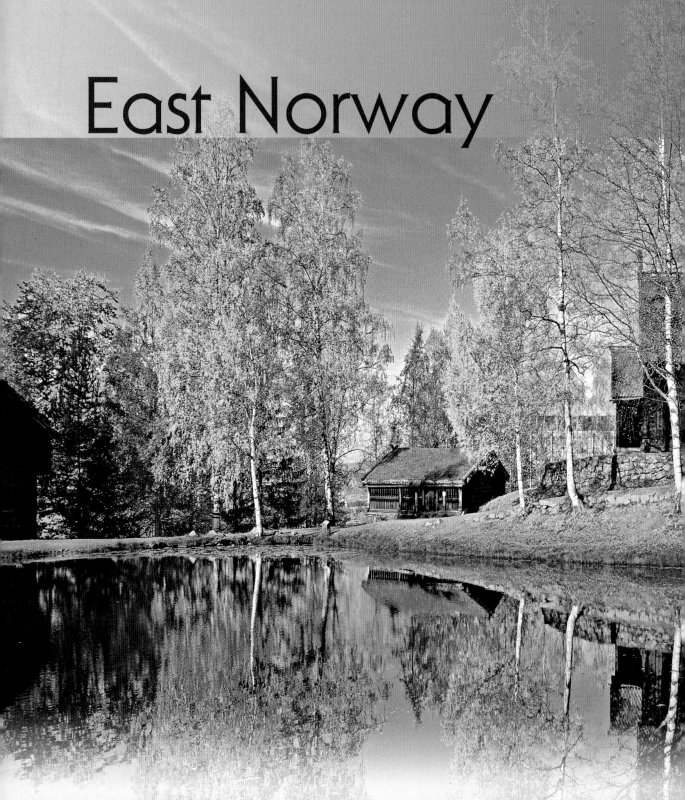

East Norway

Endless mountain plateaus, dizzying peaks and precipices, deep forests, fertile valleys, rivers and lakes teeming with fish. Irresistible challenges await skiers, ramblers, anglers, hunters, and everyone else who relishes fresh, unspoilt nature. The cul-tural heritage of East Norway also offers a wealth of exciting possibilities. Here you can discover gems of the country's unique wooden architec-ture, and sail on Lake Mjøsa on the world's oldest paddle steamer in regular service.

Lillehammer, Maihaugen

THE MOUNTAINS

Norwegians have a passion for the outdoor life. They use nature both as a sports arena and an exhilarating opportunity for recreation. For many people, the mountains hold a special attraction. They offer demanding challenges and dramatic panoramas, but also peace and harmony on the banks of a calm mountain lake.

Left: View of Gjende in the Jotunheimen.
Below left: Exploring the mountains.
Below: Autumn in Rondane.

Above: Purple mountain saxi-frage and glacier crowfoot.
Right: Reindeer buck.

FOREST COUNTRY

The endless forests of East Norway - the kingdom of the elk - offer all kinds of experiences in nature. There are excellent opportunities for hunting, and a wealth of forest berries and mush-rooms. There are rare animals living here, such as bears, wolves, and lynxes. And those with a lively imagination might catch a glimpse of a real Norwegian troll in the depths of the forests.

Left: Brown bear.
Above left: Grouse hunt.
Above right: Mushrooms from nature's pantry.
Above, far right: Blackcock.
Right: The elk - king of the forest.

Previous pages : Winter evening in the Jotunheimen.

At the northern end of Mjøsa, Norway's largest lake, is Lillehammer, a charming little city that became world famous when the Winter Olympics were held here in 1994. The city is surrounded by a superb area for hiking, and has a long history as a highly popular centre for winter sports. The traditional Birkebeinerrennet from Rena to Lillehammer is Norway's most famous long-distance cross-country skiing event.

One of the largest open-air museums in northern Europe is at Maihaugen in Lillehammer. It presents a rural society with old buildings from the entire Gudbrandsdalen valley, including the farm and the crofters' farm, the stave church and the vicarage, the summer dairies and the fishermen's shelters. The city collection with buildings from the Lillehammer area shows us an inland city from the early 20th century.

Left: Skibladner on Mjøsa, the world's oldest paddle steamer in regular operation.
Previous page, top: Maihaugen and Birkebeinerrennet.
Above: Hunderfossen Family Park.
Right: The busy street of Storgata in Lillehammer.
Below: The Viking Ship in Hamar is one of the world's largest skating halls and was an Olympic arena in 1994.

TELEMARK

Telemark has taken good care of its rich cultural heritage. The old brown Telemark houses with their distinctive building style and magnificent carvings represent some of the finest Norwegian architecture in wood. The oldest preserved Telemark houses are more than 800 years old. Forms of culture such as folk music and Norwegian rose painting still flourish in Telemark today.

Skien is the largest city in Telemark. This is the beginning of the Telemark Canal, which is more than a century old. It stretches from the coast to the mountains at the foot of the Hardangervidda mountain plateau.

Above left: Skien with the statue of Henrik Ibsen and Skien Church.

Left: The peak of Gaustatoppen, 1883 m.

Above: ”Victoria” on the Telemark Canal.

Right: Richly decorated Telemark loft house at Kviteseid Bygdetun.

Below: Rose-painted interior in Rambergstugu at Heddal Bygdetun.

The South Coast

Somewhere between the sea and the sky in the southernmost part of Norway is the summer dream of many Norwegians: Spend a lazy, sun-filled holiday discovering the islets of the South Coast. Lie on the deck of a boat, listening to the lapping waves and the cries of the seagulls as the idyllic white-painted towns and inviting beaches glide slowly past. On the quayside, enjoy sunripened strawberries and mackerel fresh from the sea, while lilting songs and accordion melodies ripple out among the islets and reefs, disappearing into the mild and mysterious night.

Brekkestø

White-painted coastal towns lie like a ring of pearls along the South Coast. These towns had their heyday at the time of the sailing ships.

Left and above: Risør - "the white town on the Skagerrak" - organizes a wooden-boat festival every year.

Above right: Lindesnes lighthouse - the southernmost point of Norway's mainland.

Right: Kardemomme by ("Cardamom Town") Kristiansand Zoo.

Following pages : The holiday paradise of Lyngør.

The South Coast is the holiday
paradise of boating enthusiasts with
sunny summer days, sea, sailing
and swimming.
The sea route between Lillesand
and Kristiansand is called Blindleia.
A boat trip here is one of the most
beautiful experiences you can have
along the South Coast. You will see
an abundance of old wooden
houses, painted white with
red-tiled roofs.

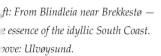

*Left: From Blindleia near Brekkestø —
the essence of the idyllic South Coast.
Above: Ulvøysund.
Right: Holiday memories from the
South Coast.*

The fjords of West Norway are the international superstars of the Norwegian landscape - admired and much visited by travellers from all over the world. Would you like to know why? Take a boat trip on the Sognefjord or Geirangerfjord on a sunny day in May, as waterfalls, wild with the energy of spring, cascade down steep mountainsides. Delight in the sparkling white mountain peaks and their reflections in the turquoise fjord. Then, travel to Kjerag. Sit on the edge of the cliff and - with intermingled joy and terror - enjoy the view of Lysefjord 1000 precipitous metres right below your feet. You'll never forget it.

West Norway

Geiranger

JÆREN

Norway's longest sandy beaches line the coast of Jæren, beside the North Sea. They border some of the largest and most fertile agricultural areas in Norway.

*Top left: The monument
"Sverd i fjell" ("Swords in Rock") in
Hafrsfjord, sculpted by Fritz Røed.
Centre left: Surfing at Jæren.
Left: Farm landscape near Klepp.
Above. Storm clouds loom over the Jæren
coastline near the Feistein lighthouse.
Right: Swimming at Solastranden.*

STAVANGER

The Vågen harbour area is at the heart of Stavanger's close-knit and picturesque central area. The city is a natural starting point for boat trips on the dramatic Lysefjord, where the rock formations of Preikestolen (Pulpit Rock) and Kjerag are the most impressive sights.
Close to Stavanger is Jæren, with its flat, fertile farmlands and endless sandy beaches. In recent years Stavanger has grown rapidly as a result of Norway's oil operations in the North Sea.

Right: Gamle Stavanger (Old Stavanger).
Below and below right: The wharves along
Vågen and the Valberg tower (Valbergtårnet).

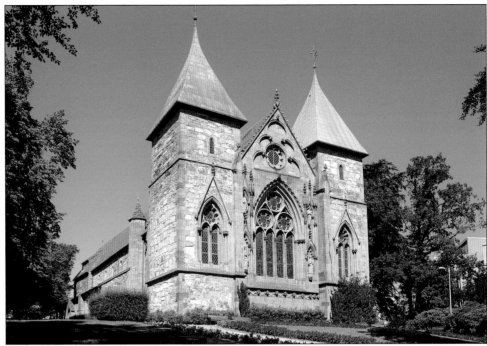

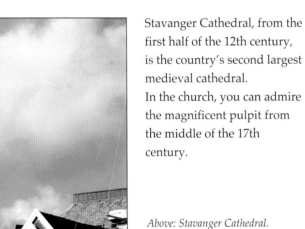

Stavanger Cathedral, from the first half of the 12th century, is the country's second largest medieval cathedral.
In the church, you can admire the magnificent pulpit from the middle of the 17th century.

Above: Stavanger Cathedral.
Right: Interior from Stavanger Cathedral.

PREIKESTOLEN AND KJERAG

Preikestolen – "Pulpit Rock" – is the most
famous tourist attraction in Rogaland.
Together with Kjerag, further along the
Lysefjord, Preikestolen is dizzyingly steep.
Preikestolen is 604 m and Kjerag 1084 m.

Above left: Kjeragbolten.
Above: View towards Kjerag and the Lysefjord.
Left: Kjerag is a popular location for base jumpers.
Below: On the brink of the precipice: view from
Preikestolen. Right: Preikestolen – "Pulpit Rock".

Hardanger is Norway's orchard. Delectable apples, pears and cherries grow on the sunny banks of the Hardangerfjord. Spring in Hardanger is an enchanting symphony of colour: a sea of pink apple blossom surrounded by snow-clad peaks, green meadows and blue fjords.

Left: The Vøringfossen waterfall in Måbødalen. Above: Apples and apple blossom. Right: Girl in Hardanger national costume. Below: The idyllic Hardangerfjord.

BERGEN

Bergen is the gateway to the fjord kingdom of West Norway. The city was founded by King Olav Kyrre in 1070, and in the High Middle Ages it was Scandinavia's most important trade and shipping centre.

The architecture of Bergen offers an exciting diversity of styles – the city centre is characterized by a charming mixture of old and new buildings. Towering commercial blocks are intermingled with entrancing alleyways.

After taking the Fløibanen funicular up to Fløyen (320 m or 1050 feet) you can enjoy the magnificent view over the city and the inner harbour, Vågen, with the fjords and the sea in the background.

o find the soul of the city, wander
longside the old warehouses of the
ryggen overlooking the harbour. Their
istinctive façade is Bergen's hallmark.
hese historic merchant buildings were
nce the centre of the Hanseatic League's
ubstantial trade in Norway, and are listed
s a UNESCO World Heritage Site.

eft: The Fløibanen funicular.
op left: Strangebakken, Nordnes.
bove: The old trading district of Bryggen.
ight: The Church of Maria from the 12th century.
elow: The bandstand.

n warm summer evenings, the ambience in Bergen is almost
Mediterranean. There is a bustle of life along the Vågen, and
the city's many outdoor restaurants are filled to capacity.

Left: View over Vågen. Above: From Torgalmenningen.
Right: Fantoft Stave Church – a copy of the old stave church from
Fortun in Sogn (built ca. 1150).
Below: View over Vågen, Bryggen, and the fish market.

Idyllic Troldhaugen on the outskirts of Bergen is the home of the Edvard Grieg Museum, with the composer's house, the cabin where he wrote his music, and a modern chamber music hall, Troldsalen. Concerts are held here throughout the summer season.

nermost in the Vågen harbour is the pulsing heart
Bergen - the fish market. The colourful awnings
ade an abundant diversity of fresh fish.High over
e town towers the Ulriken mountain (642m above
a level).
e Ulriksbanen cable car takes you up to this
pular viewpoint.

ft: Statue of Edvard Grieg, and the composer's
use at Troldhaugen.
low left: Bryggen, Fløyen and Ulriken.
ght: Ulriksbanen. Below: The fish market.

The Sognefjord is Norway's longest and the world's second longest fjord. It stretches inland for more than 200 km (120 miles) – all the way to the Jostedalsbreen glacier and the Jotunheimen mountains. The fjord takes us through wild and dramatic landscapes, lush farmland, and cultural relics from the past.

Left: Mowing – the good old way.
Below: The Feigumfoss waterfall near the Sognefjord, one of the highest waterfalls in Norway.
Right: Bergsetbreen in Jostedalen, an arm of the Jostedalsbreen glacier.

FLÅM AND AURLAND

Aurlandsfjord is an arm of the Sogne fjord, where the villages of Aurland and Flåm are located. English and German tourists were already starting to explore this dramatic fjord landscape at the end of the 19th century. Today, Flåm is a busy cruise port in the summer half-year. Flåm is the starting point for the Flåm Railway, one of the most spectacular railway lines in the world.

Left: Cruise ship in Flåm.
Below: View over Aurland and Aurlandsfjord. Below left: The Flåm Railway and Flåm church.
Right: From the beautiful Flåmsdalen valley.

NÆRØYFJORD

This arm of Sognefjord is framed by steep mountainsides with impressive waterfalls, narrow valleys and small patches of idyllic farmland.

Both Nærøyfjord and Geirangerfjord are included in UNESCO's prestigious World Heritage List as representatives of the unique Norwegian fjord landscape. A boat trip on Nærøyfjord on a sunny day offers unparalleled vistas of nature.

Top left: Nærøyfjord.
Above: Tourists sailing along Nærøyfjord.
Right: The tiny village of Bakka on the banks of the Nærøyfjord.

BRIKSDAL GLACIER

ostedalsbreen is the largest glacier on the European mainland. Briksdal Glacier is the most famous arm of the larger glacier. From a height of 1200m (nearly 4000 ft), the wild icefall plunges all the way down into the lush Briksdalen valley. People from all over the world seek out this unique gem of nature. Briksdal Glacier is one of Norway's most popular tourist attractions.

Far left: Tourists on the way up to the glacier.
Centre left: Glacier hiking. Left: Horse-drawn ride.
Below: Briksdal Glacier and Briksdal Lake.
Right: Aerial view of the icefall. Bottom right: Briksdal Waterfall.

The landscape of the Jostedalsbreen National Park offers fascinating contrasts. Luxuriant meadows studded with flowers grow up to the edges of impressive glacier arms, and romantic clusters of mountain farms are reflected in calm water surrounded by towering peaks.

Many tourists make their way to the natural beauty of the areas around Stryn, Loen, Olden and Jølster – a travel destination with a wealth of tradition. The Strynefjellsveien road links Stryn with the villages of Skjåk and Lom in south-east Norway.

Left: Flock of goats near Kjøsnes Fjord.
Below: View towards the Hjelledalen valley from Gamle Strynefjellsvei.

Above: Mountain farms overlooking the lake of ...envatn. Right: Girls in national dress near the ...stravatnet lake.

EIRANGERFJORD

eiranger is one of the world's most famous travel
estinations. Enchanting waterfalls along the fjord
clude Friaren (the Suitor), De Syv Søstre (the
even Sisters), and Brudesløret (the Bridal Veil).
ourists are also impressed by the many small
rms perched on the mountainsides. Geiranger-
ord has been listed as a UNESCO World
eritage Site because of its unique natural beauty
d cultural landscape.

*ft: View of Geirangerfjord and the Seven Sisters waterfall
m the mountain farm of Skageflå.*
bove: Viewpoint at the Ørneveien road.
ght: Flydalsjuvet Gorge.
*ottom: Tourist bus negotiating the hairpin bends of the
rrow Geiranger Road.*

Above: Ålesund seen from Aksla.
Left: Brosundet. Below: Detail from the
Art Nouveau architecture.

LESUND

fter the great fire of 1904, the
wn was rebuilt in the
chitectural style of the period,
rt Nouveau, inspired by the
erman Jugendstil movement.
lesund is one of the few pre-
rved Jugendstil towns in the
orld. From the centre, a path
ads up to the Aksla peak. Here,
ou have a superb view of the
wn, the sea and the Sunnmøre
ps.

*p right: View of the Hjørund
ord, Sunnmøre.*

ntre right: Herdalseter Farm.

*ght: Atlanterhavsparken, outside
esund, is one of Northern Europe's
gest saltwater aquariums.*

TROLLSTIGEN AND TROLLVEGGEN

The awe-inspiring mountains of the north-west coast lure those who seek nature's exciting challenges. Trollveggen in Romsdalen with its dizzying 1000-metre precipice attracts mountain climbers from all over the world.

Trollstigen is the most famous tourist road in Norway. It is easy to understand why. The road winds up precipitou mountainsides and offers the thrill of "mountain climbing on wheels". At the top, a breathtaking view is your reward. The Trollstigen Road is framed by the majestic Romsdalsfje mountains. Keep your camera handy!

are the mountains known as the Bishop, the King
d the Queen.
ght: View from Store Trolltind in Trolltindan
vards Trollveggen and Romsdalen.
ow right: Trollveggen seen from Romsdalen.

81

ATLANTERHAVSVEIEN – THE ATLANTIC OCEAN ROAD

One of Norway's most spectacular roads links Kristiansund and Molde. With its eight bridges, the Atlantic Ocean Road winds from island to island with the ocean as its nearest neighbour. Driving along the Atlantic Ocean Road can be a dramatic experience during the storms of autumn.

Above left: Molde Church.
Below: The idyllic fishing village of Bud.

Right: The Atlantic Ocean Road in stormy weather. Below right: Aerial view of the Atlantic Ocean Road.

Here, history lives on. The imposing tower and spire of Nidaros Cathedral soar silhouetted against Trondheim's evening sky. The sonorous tones of the bell in Scandinavia's largest medieval building ring out over Norway's first capital city. The cathedral is the most dazzling jewel in the treasure chest of Trøndelag County, but there are more riches to discover. Some of the best salmon rivers in the country wind like silver ribbons through Central Norway's mild and tranquil landscape, and golden cornfields ripple in the breeze. The Dovrefjell massif crowns the southernmost part of the region.

Central Norway

Trondheim.

Previous pages: Musk oxen on Dovrefjell.

WINTER

Winter and snow abound in
Norway. On occasion, Norwegians
think that there is more than
enough … Fine winter days tempt
many people to go skiing in the
inviting and beautiful countryside.
Skiing is Norway's national sport.

THE MINING TOWN OF RØROS

The old mining town of Røros with its unique wooden buildings has a well-deserved place on UNESCO's World Heritage List. The distinctive tower of "Bergstadens Ziir" – Røros Church, dating from 1784 – is a landmark of the town. The second to last Tuesday in February every year marks the opening of Rørosmartnan, a five-day market with long traditions in the town. The market was held for the first time in 1854. In the old days it was primarily a horse and hide market, where people from Sweden and the neighbouring villages arrived to gather and to trade. Lively bargaining and bustling crowds still characterize the market today. A wealth of cultural activities takes place in community halls and cafés.

Above and left: From Rørosmartnan.
Top right: The characteristic
old wooden buildings, Slagghaugen
and Røros Church.
Right (centre): Winter night. Full moon
over Røros Church. Bottom right: Folk
dancing on Aasen Farm.

TRONDHEIM

According to the saga writer Snorre Sturlason, Olav Tryggvason founded
the city in 997. Trondheim was the capital of the country for
much of the Middle Ages, and offers a wealth of historical sights.
Cultural life flourishes in Trondheim, and several large festivals take
place every year. The St. Olav Festival is the most famous. It celebrates
the memory of King Olav the Holy.
The city has developed into one of Norway's largest university towns,
and is an important centre of advanced technological research.

Bottom left: Bakklandet
Below: The market square with the sundial and the statue of Olav Tryggvason.
Above left: The Tyholt Tower. Above right: Munkholmen.
Bottom right: Gamle Bybro (the old town bridge), Bakklandet and Kristiansten Fortress.

THE NIDAROS CATHEDRAL

This magnificent cathedral is Norway's national sanctuary, and the largest medieval building in Scandinavia. The church was built over the grave of the saint-king Olav Haraldson, who fell in the battle of Stiklestad on 29 July 1030. In the Middle Ages, Nidaros Cathedral was one of the four most popular destinations for pilgrimages. The others were Jerusalem, Rome, and Santiago de Compostela.

Left: Aerial view of Trondheim.   *Right and below: Nidaros Cathedral.*

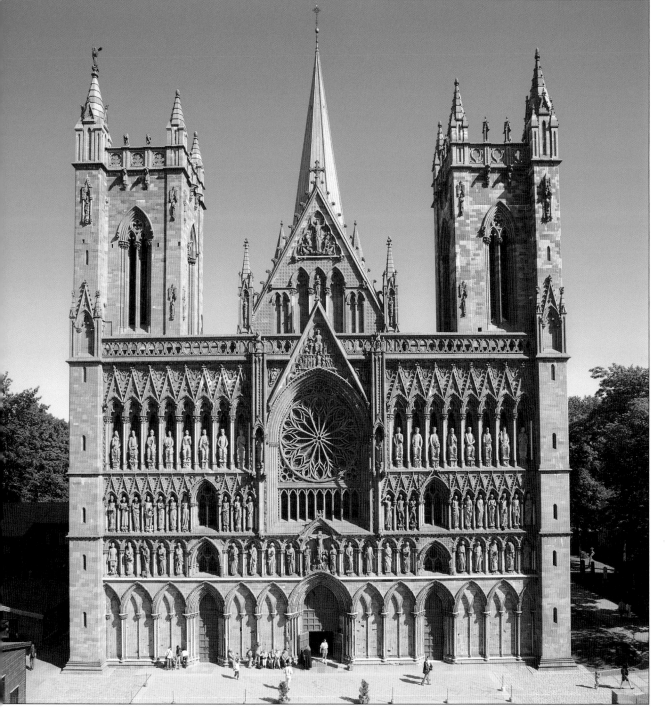

95

Some of Norway's most fertile farmland areas are located along the Trondheims-fjord. They conjure up the atmosphere of a dramatic past.

The cultural landscape of Trøndelag has a rich historical heritage.

Top left: The wharves of Råkvåg in Fosen.
Above: Austrått Castle, Ørlandet.
Below: Farmland in Verdal.
Right: Steinvikholmen Castle near Stjørdal.

North Norway

With irrepressible optimism, Northern Norway defies the cold, merciless Arctic ocean and rashly reaches toward the North Pole. Why do people live here so far north of the Arctic Circle? Ask those born here, and they will describe the region with sparkling enthusiasm: This is an exciting place, rich in opportunities! A constantly changing and fascinating light reveals a unique and magnificent landscape. The biting snowstorms and the darkness of winter are forgotten when summer breathes the gentle warmth of the southerly wind over fjords and mountains, as the midnight sun glows over the sea.

Vestvågøy, Lofoten

A voyage on the Hurtigruten ship along the Helgeland coast leads you into a fascinating world of islands and mountains rich in myths and legends. Some of Norway's most well-known legends are associated with the mountains De syv søstre (the Seven Sisters) and Torghatten. Far out in the ocean, just below the Arctic Circle, lies the distinctive fishing village of Træna. The Vega Archipelago on the Helgeland coast is listed as a UNESCO World Heritage Site because of its unique cultural value.

Top left: The mountain of Torghatten. Left (centre): Træna. Left: The Hurtigruten ship and the Seven Sisters. Above: Engabreen – part of the Svartisen Glacier. Right: The Polarsirkelsenteret (Arctic Circle Centre) at Saltfjellet.

Right: Kjerringøy.   Below: White-tailed sea eagle.
Bottom: Saltstraumen and Børvasstindan.

Bodø can justifiably be called the city of sea-eagles. No other city in the world has such a large population of white-tailed sea eagles. Bodø is northern Norway's second largest cit and the capital of Nordland County. North o Bodø lies idyllic Kjerringøy, with the coast's best preserved trading post from the 19th century. Just east of Bodø is the maelstrom o Saltstraumen, which is the world's strongest tidal current and a paradise for anglers.

arvik's history is closely linked to the large iron-
re reserves in Swedish Lapland. In 1898 work
arted on the Ofot railway, which made it possible
transport the ore from Kiruna in Sweden to the
e-free port in Narvik. The construction work was
ruelling, especially on the Norwegian side, where
e line had to be carved out of the precipitous
ountainsides. The line, 168 km (104 miles) long,
as completed in 1902. Every year in February /
larch, Narvik celebrates the Winter Festival Week
honour of those who built the line: the railway
orkers and Svarta Bjørn – the beautiful cook.

bove left: The "Rallaren" (railway worker) statue in Narvik.
bove right: The cableway in Narvik.
ight: Ferry on the Ofotfjord with the peak of Stetind in the
ckground.
elow: The Midnight Sun near Landegode, north of Bodø.

LOFOTEN AND VESTERÅLEN

Everyone who visits Lofoten and Vesterålen is captivated by the dramatic landscape - a magical mixture of precipitous mountains, picturesque fishing villages, the glow of the midnight sun, and flourishing farmland.

These islands lure a growing number of travellers in search of adventure. Here you can go fishing with weathered Lofot fishermen, see the amazing rich variety of bird life in the large nesting cliffs, or join a whale safari. Climb one of the many peaks which are wreathed in legend. A breathtaking panorama is the reward for your efforts.

op left: The idyllic old fishing village of Å. Bottom left: The village
Nusfjord on Flakstadøy.
bove: Sandy beaches near Leknes on Vestvågøy.
ight: Svolvær, with the Svolværgeita rock formation ("the Goat")
the foreground.
elow: View of Reine, on the island of Moskenesøy.

Left: The fishing grounds.
Above: Seagull.
Right: A genuine Lofoten cod.
Far right: Fish drying on racks.
Below: Fishing boats in the harbour,
Henningsvær.

OFOTEN FISHING SEASON

he Lofoten fishing season lasts om January to April. Fishing r spawning cod is an impor-nt industry with a long story, rich in tradition. The dest way of processing fish — drying the cod on racks — is ll common. In the Middle ges, dried fish from Lofoten as Norway's most important port.

shing and related industries main important to the Lofoten d Vesterålen islands.

To the north of Lofoten Islands are the islands of Vesterålen, with a gentler landscape and expansive stretches of farm-land. Overlooking the ocean, the fishing town of Andenes is at the northern end of Andøya. This is a starting point for whale safaris – a highly popular activity for many tourists.

Previous page: The Hurtigruten ship in Trollfjord.
This page, top left: The midnight sun over Nykan and the wharves in Nyksund. This page, above: The old vicarage of Hadsel with the mountain Møysalen in the background.
This page, left: Whale safari.
This page, below: Andenes and Atlantic puffin.

Farmers from Østerdalen and Gudbrandsdalen migrated to the fertile countryside of Indre Troms at the end of the 18th century. The extensive wilderness areas in the county of Troms are a great attraction for those who love the outdoor life.

lselva, one of Norway's largest
mon rivers, runs through the
;ion. The national parks of Øvre
vidalen and Reisa are also located
re.

e majestic Lyngen Alps soar from
· Lyngenfjord, with Jiehkkevarri
33 m) as the highest peak. Lyngen
ers many exciting challenges for
nblers and mountain climbers.

vious page, top left: Målselvfossen.
vious page, top right: Salmon fishing
r the Målselvfossen waterfall.
vious page, bottom: Otertind in the
naldalen valley.

This page, top left: Mountain climbers at the top of Store Lenangstind.
This page, above: Winter night in Balsfjord. This page, below: Lyngenfjord.

TROMSØ

Tromsø - the Gateway to the Arctic - is the largest town in North Norway. Fishing, trapping and trade formed the foundation for the city.
Close to the Arctic Ocean, Tromsø was a natural starting-point for polar expeditions. The names of famous explorers such as Roald Amundsen, Fridtjof Nansen and Umerto Nobile are inextricably linked with Tromsø. The University of Tromsø is the most northerly university in the world.

Previous page, top: The Hurtigruten ship, Tromsø Bridge, Arctic Ocean Cathedral and the peak of Tromsdalstind.
This page, top left: Wharves north of Torghuken, with the Polar Museum at the far right.
This page, above left: The statue of Roald Amundsen and the Arctic Ocean Cathedral.
This page, top right: The cableway.
Left: The sun and the light disappear in the south - the Arctic night falls slowly over Tromsø.

Have you ever stood outside in the North Norwegian winter night and marvelled at the dancing light high up in the dark blue sky? Have you been fascinated by the colourful spectacle of Arctic nature, where the night-black ocean and the white, snow-clad mountain tops create powerful and dramatic backdrops? You are not alone. A growing number of people travel long distances to experience the breathtaking "Theatre of Lights" in the Arctic night. This celestial phenomenon has always captured human imagination, and many myths, mysteries and superstitions enshroud the Northern Lights. Our ancestors often associated the northern lights with danger and misfortune. Some believed that these flickering lights were the spirits of dead virgins in the dark night sky, dancing and enticing those who watched them.

What are the northern lights? Powerful explosions in the sun cast large volumes of energy-charged electrical particles towards earth. Where these particles interact with the earth's atmosphere, the northern lights appear. The phenomenon occurs most often and most intensely in a belt around the earth's magnetic poles. The northern lights constantly change in shape, colour and strength. The greenish-yellow northern lights are perhaps the most common, but white, red, blue and mauve colours also occur fairly often.

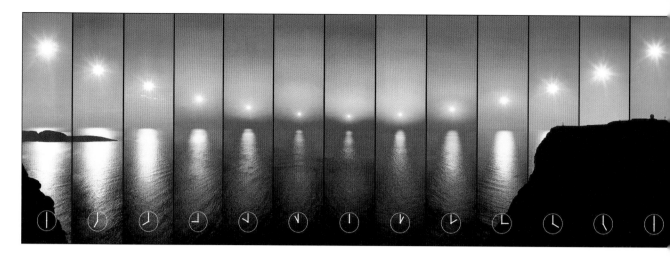

NORDKAPP

"Here I am now at the North Cape, which is the outermost limit of Finnmark, and I might well say, of the whole world... My curiosity is now satisfied, and I am prepared to return ...God willing, to my own country."
Francesco Negri, 1664.

North Cape is Europe's northern spearhead. The dramatic cliff that plunges 307 metres into the Arctic Ocean is a popular tourist attraction. Each year, more than 200,000 people from all over the world visit North Cape. Most of them dream of seeing the world-famous rock in the magical light of the midnight sun. Weather permitting, you can see the midnight sun here from 14 May to 30 July.

The midnight sun seen from North Cape, 71°10'21".
This panoramic view of Knivskjellodden, the Arctic Ocean and t North Cape rock shows the path of the sun from 6 p.m. to 6 a.

Below: The Kirkeporten rock formation near Skarsvå
Below left: The globe on the extremity of the North Cape platea
Below right: The sculpture group "Children of the Earth
Next page: North Cape profi

FINNMARK

Finnmark offers vast expanses of untouched nature. The Finnmarksvidda plateau is the largest continuous wilderness area in Europe. Only 75,000 people live in this region, which is considerably larger than Denmark. With their colourful costumes and rich cultural heritage, the Sami people of Finnmark represent a striking and exotic contrast to the Norwegian community. Herding reindeer was the traditional occupation of the Sami, who wandered with their animals along time-worn paths between the winter pastures of Finnmarksvidda and the summer grazing near the coast. Today, only a few Sami still make their living this way. The Sami culture has flourished in recent years.

Left: At Sautso, the river Altaelva has carved out the largest canyon in northern Europe.

On the windswept Finnmark coast, we find Hammerfest and Honningsvåg, the world's northernmost urban settlements. Melkøya near Hammerfest is the base for landing the large volumes of natural gas from the Snøhvit field in the Barents Sea.

Further inland, at the mouth of the Alta river, is Alta, which has grown into Finnmark's most populous town. Hammerfest and Vardø are the oldest towns in northern Norway, with city status from 1789. Vardø is the country's easternmost city, and Vardøhus Festning from 1738 is the world's northernmost historical fortress.

Left: Hammerfest. Previous page, bottom: Honningsvåg.
Below, left King Oscar II's Chapel, Grense Jakobselv.
Below, right: King crab – Paralithodes camtschatica.
Bottom left: Vardøhus Fortress.
Bottom right: Close to Alta Museum you can see the largest and richest field of prehistoric rock carvings in northern Europe. The carvings are listed as a UNESCO World Heritage Site.

Svalbard

Eternal ice cover most of Svalbard, "the Land of the cold coasts" Norway's exotic outpost in the Arctic. This is the kingdom of the polar bear. Be warned: it may appear where you least expect it. Desolate though the nature of the Arctic may seem, it radiates an icy beauty that many people find spellbinding. Impressive mountains, fjords and glaciers make their mark on the landscape. The short, hectic summer of Svalbard conjures up flowers in glorious colours, contrasting starkly with their barren surroundings. Svalbard also offers a surprising wealth of birds and animals.

Longyearbyen

ARCTIC NORWAY

There are two things that everyone who has visited Longyearbyen, the main settlement of Svalbard, will remember: The stunning and distinctive landscape leaves a deep impression on you - and so does the sign warning you to beware of the polar bears. Everyone who ventures beyond the central settlements should take a firearm with them.

The largest settlements after Longyearbyen are Ny-Ålesund and Barentsburg. Coal mining and trapping were the historical ways of making a living on Svalbard. The mountains still yield coal, but in recent years research activities and tourism have become increasingly important. A small arm of the Gulf Stream keeps the west coast of Spitsbergen open for shipping during the summer. This is the most northerly ice-free coast in the world, and the northern frontier for most plant, animal and bird life on our planet.

The permafrost ecology is extremely vulnerable, and demands care and consideration from the tourists who wander here. To preserve Svalbard's unique Arctic nature, 60 per cent of the archipelago is protected as national parks and nature reserves.

Above right: Polar bear, Tempelfjorden.

Above centre: Moss campion.

Above: Svalbard reindeer. Left: Longyearbyen.

NORWAY

FACTS ABOUT NORWAY

Area including
Svalbard and Jan Mayen:
387,000 km²

Population:
Approx. 4,800,000

System of government:
Constitutional monarchy

State religion:
Protestant Christianity

Population of the largest
five cities:

Oslo:	575,000
Bergen:	250,000
Trondheim:	168,000
Stavanger:	122,000
Kristiansand:	79,000

Length of the mainland coast:
Approx. 21,500 km

Highest mountain:
Galdhøpiggen 2,469 m

Largest island:
Hinnøya 2,198 km²

Longest fjord:
Sognefjorden 204 km

Largest lake:
Mjøsa 362 km²

Longest river:
Glomma 600 km

Highest waterfall:
Brudesløret, Geiranger 300

Largest glacier:
Jostedalsbreen 487 km²

This book is published by
AUNE FORLAG AS
Lade Allé 63
P.O.Box 1808 Lade
N-7440 Trondheim
Telephone: +47 73 82 83 00
Telefax: +47 73 82 83 01
E-mail: **firmapost@aune-forlag.no**
Internet: **www.aune-forlag.no**

Text:
**Ole P. Rørvik and
Ole Magnus Rapp**

Design:
Aune Forlag AS

Cartography, page 128:
Cartographica AS

Printing: **BookPrint AS**

English translation: **Margaret Forbes**
German translation: **Carola Peckolt**
French translation: **Nadine Haudecoeur**
Italian translation: **Federico Venzi**
Spanish translation: **Ivar Evjenth**
Russian translation: **Noricom**
Dutch translation: **Noricom**

Photographs by:
Aune Forlag / Ole P. Rørvik

Additional photpgraphs by:
Trond Aalde: 1
Frode Jenssen: 2-3
Otto Frengen: 5CE
Universitetets Oldsaksamling:
8CD, 28CD
Scanpix: 9AE, 9CD, 10AE, 10BD,
10BE, 10CD, 11AD
Kon-Tiki Museet: 10CE, 28CE
Nationalgalleriet: 11AE
Edvard Grieg Museum: 11CD
Arne Aas: 12AE, 12BE, 12CE, 43CE
Aune Forlag/Kolbjørn Dekkerhus:
13A, 46, 47CE, 49C, 74A, 75C, 90,
91AE, 91BE
Per Eide/Samfoto: 14AE, 15CD,
15CE, 57A, 57CD, 59C, 79BE
Torbjørn Moen: 14C
Erik Berg/Den Norske Opera & Ballett:
24CE, 25AD
JDS Architects: 29AE
Rune Lislerud/Samfoto: 30AE
Tore Sandberg: 30BE
Svein Grønvold: 31A
Bård Løken/Samfoto: 34A, 35AE,
36-37, 83A
Espen Bratlie/Samfoto: 34CD,39AD
79C
Bjarne Riesto: 35AD
Johannes Haugan/Samfoto: 35AB
Arnfinn Pedersen: 35C
Tommy Solberg: 38A
Nils Sundberg: 38C
Kjell Erik Moseid: 39AE, 39C
Giulio Bolognesi: 40AD, 40C, 78CE
Jørgen Skaug: 40AE
Ove Bergersen/Samfoto: 42C, 43A
Terje Rakke: 49AE

Jostein Moene: 52BD
Ole Endresen: 53A
Olav Breen: 56AD
Tom Schandy/Samfoto: 56C
Stig Tronvold/Samfoto: 59AD,
105A
Helge Sunde/Samfoto: 63AE, 66A
Robin Strand: 65A
Vidar Moløkken: 70AD, 81AE
Finn Loftesnes: 72AB
Jarle Wæhler/Opplandsbilder:
77AD, 77C
Christian Dybvik: 78A
Gunnar Wangen: 79AE
Øystein Søbye/Samfoto: 86-87
Ragnar Ness: 88AD
Steve Halsetrønning/Samfoto:
88AE
Arne Tønset: 88CD, 91C
Simen Berg: 89A
Jon Arne Sæter: 102A
Roy Mangersnes: 102B
Aune Forlag/Knut Aune:103C
Frithjof Fure: 104A
Tore Wuttudal/Samfoto: 107AD,
109CE
Hanne Strager: 109B
Arthur Kjelstrup-Olsen:113AD
Aune Forlag/Roald Benjaminsen:
113AE
Bjørn Jørgensen: 114C, 116-117
Øivind Leren: 120AE
Leif Gunnar Mortensen: 122A
Jan Kåre Monsen: 123BE
Torfinn Kjærnet: 124-125, 126,
127CE
Heinrich Eggenfellner: 127A
Georg Bangjord: 127BE

Picture references:
A=above, B=centre, C=below,
D=left and E=right